EMMANUEL JOSEPH

The Infinite Library, How Literature and Psychology Decode the Mysteries of the Cosmos

Copyright © 2025 by Emmanuel Joseph

All rights reserved. No part of this publication may be reproduced, stored or transmitted in any form or by any means, electronic, mechanical, photocopying, recording, scanning, or otherwise without written permission from the publisher. It is illegal to copy this book, post it to a website, or distribute it by any other means without permission.

First edition

This book was professionally typeset on Reedsy.
Find out more at reedsy.com

Contents

1	Chapter 1: The Opening Pages: A Universe in Words	1
2	Chapter 2: The Psychology of Storytelling: Unraveling the...	3
3	Chapter 3: Myth and Meaning: Ancient Narratives and Cosmic...	5
4	Chapter 4: The Labyrinth of the Mind: Psychological...	7
5	Chapter 5: Cosmic Symbolism: The Universe in Metaphor	9
6	Chapter 6: The Interstellar Imagination: Science Fiction and...	11
7	Chapter 7: The Cosmic Dance: Literature and Quantum...	13
8	Chapter 8: The Poetry of the Stars: Celestial Imagery in...	15
9	Chapter 9: Dreams and the Night Sky: Unveiling the...	17
10	Chapter 10: The Language of the Universe: Symbols and...	19
11	Chapter 11: The Infinite Possibilities: Literature,...	21
12	Chapter 12: The Final Chapter: Reflecting on the Infinite...	23
13	Chapter 13: The Harmony of the Spheres: Music, Literature,...	25
14	Chapter 14: The Alchemy of Words: Literature and the...	27
15	Chapter 15: The Cosmos Within: Inner Space and the...	29

1

Chapter 1: The Opening Pages: A Universe in Words

The universe can be an overwhelming concept to grasp, its mysteries vast and seemingly impenetrable. Yet, through literature, humanity has always sought to make sense of the cosmos. Stories and mythologies across cultures have woven narratives about the stars, the origins of life, and our place within the grand scheme of things. From the ancient epics of Homer's "Iliad" and "Odyssey" to contemporary science fiction, literature serves as a bridge, connecting our imagination to the universe's enigmas. These tales, laden with symbolism and metaphor, often mirror our innermost psychological landscapes, reflecting the fears, aspirations, and quests for understanding that define the human experience.

Literary works do more than merely describe the world around us; they dive into the human psyche, exploring the depths of our consciousness. Carl Jung's theory of archetypes, for instance, suggests that recurring characters and themes in literature tap into universal aspects of the human experience. By decoding these archetypes, we gain insights into the shared unconscious that binds humanity. Literature, therefore, is not just a tool for entertainment but a profound instrument for self-discovery and cosmic comprehension. It allows us to confront the unknown, whether it be the vastness of space or the intricacies of the human mind.

Moreover, literature's power to evoke emotions plays a crucial role in this exploration. When we read a story, we don't just process information; we feel the characters' joys and sorrows, their triumphs and defeats. These emotional journeys mirror our psychological processes, making literature a therapeutic conduit for exploring our inner worlds. By engaging with diverse narratives, we open ourselves to new perspectives and experiences, enhancing our empathy and understanding of the universe's complexities.

Finally, literature's capacity for metaphor allows us to grapple with abstract concepts in a tangible way. Metaphors like "the fabric of the cosmos" or "the dance of the planets" turn scientific phenomena into relatable imagery. These literary devices enrich our comprehension of the universe, making it more accessible and less daunting. Thus, the opening pages of our exploration reveal that literature is not just a passive reflection of the cosmos but an active participant in decoding its mysteries, blending the realms of imagination and reality into a cohesive whole.

2

Chapter 2: The Psychology of Storytelling: Unraveling the Human Mind

At the heart of storytelling lies the intricate tapestry of the human mind. Psychology offers invaluable tools for understanding how and why we create and consume stories. Sigmund Freud, the father of psychoanalysis, posited that narratives often serve as a window into our subconscious desires and fears. By examining literary works through a psychological lens, we can uncover hidden motivations and conflicts that shape human behavior. For instance, Freud's concept of the Oedipus complex has been used to interpret characters' actions and relationships in various literary texts, revealing deeper layers of meaning and insight.

Carl Jung expanded on Freud's ideas, introducing the notion of the collective unconscious—a reservoir of shared memories and archetypes common to all humanity. These archetypes manifest in literature as recurring symbols, characters, and themes. The hero's journey, as described by Joseph Campbell, is a prime example of an archetypal narrative that resonates across cultures and epochs. By identifying and analyzing these universal patterns, we gain a better understanding of the psychological processes that underlie storytelling. Literature becomes a mirror reflecting the collective psyche, offering clues to our shared human experience.

The act of storytelling also serves as a psychological mechanism for coping with life's uncertainties and challenges. Through narrative, we impose order on chaos, creating a sense of coherence and meaning. Viktor Frankl, a renowned psychiatrist and Holocaust survivor, emphasized the importance of finding purpose in adversity. Literature, with its diverse array of narratives, provides a rich source of inspiration and solace. Characters who overcome obstacles and achieve redemption offer readers a model for resilience and hope, fostering psychological well-being.

Furthermore, contemporary psychology recognizes the therapeutic potential of engaging with literature. Bibliotherapy, the practice of using books for healing, leverages the power of stories to address mental health issues. Through reading, individuals can gain insights into their own struggles, identify with characters, and find comfort in shared experiences. Literature becomes a safe space for exploring complex emotions and navigating the intricacies of the human mind. As we delve into the psychology of storytelling, we uncover a profound connection between literature and the human psyche, revealing the transformative power of narratives in shaping our understanding of ourselves and the cosmos.

3

Chapter 3: Myth and Meaning: Ancient Narratives and Cosmic Questions

Mythology, with its timeless tales and legendary heroes, has long served as humanity's attempt to explain the cosmos and our place within it. These ancient narratives, passed down through generations, are more than mere folklore; they are profound explorations of existential questions and universal truths. From the creation myths of different cultures to the epic sagas of gods and mortals, mythology provides a rich tapestry of stories that reflect our quest for understanding. By examining these myths, we gain insights into the psychological and philosophical underpinnings of human thought.

In Greek mythology, for instance, the story of Prometheus stealing fire from the gods symbolizes humanity's insatiable curiosity and desire for knowledge. This myth not only explains the origins of fire but also highlights the eternal struggle between innovation and the consequences of challenging the status quo. Similarly, the Norse myth of Yggdrasil, the World Tree, encapsulates the interconnectedness of all life and the cyclical nature of existence. These myths, with their intricate symbolism and allegory, offer a glimpse into the human psyche, revealing our deepest fears, hopes, and aspirations.

The universality of certain mythological themes suggests a shared human experience that transcends cultural boundaries. The hero's journey, as articulated by Joseph Campbell, is a prime example of a narrative pattern that appears in myths across the world. This journey, with its stages of departure, initiation, and return, mirrors the psychological process of personal growth and transformation. By recognizing these commonalities, we can better understand the fundamental aspects of human nature and our collective quest for meaning.

Moreover, mythology serves as a bridge between the known and the unknown, providing a framework for interpreting the mysteries of the cosmos. The Egyptian myth of Ra's journey through the underworld, for instance, represents the daily cycle of the sun and the eternal struggle between light and darkness. These myths offer a poetic lens through which we can explore astronomical phenomena, blending scientific observation with imaginative storytelling. As we delve into the rich world of mythology, we uncover a treasure trove of wisdom that illuminates our understanding of the universe and our place within it.

4

Chapter 4: The Labyrinth of the Mind: Psychological Landscapes in Literature

Literature has the unique ability to take us on journeys through the labyrinth of the human mind, exploring the intricate landscapes of thought, emotion, and consciousness. From the stream-of-consciousness narratives of James Joyce and Virginia Woolf to the psychological thrillers of Dostoevsky and Kafka, authors have long sought to capture the complexities of the inner world. These literary works offer readers a glimpse into the multifaceted nature of human psychology, revealing the depths of our fears, desires, and conflicts.

Stream-of-consciousness writing, pioneered by authors like James Joyce in "Ulysses," immerses readers in the continuous flow of a character's thoughts and perceptions. This narrative technique provides an intimate portrayal of the mind's workings, highlighting the fragmented and nonlinear nature of consciousness. By delving into these literary landscapes, readers gain a deeper appreciation for the richness and complexity of human experience, as well as the psychological processes that shape our perceptions and actions.

Psychological thrillers, on the other hand, often explore the darker aspects of the human psyche, delving into themes of madness, obsession, and moral ambiguity. Fyodor Dostoevsky's "Crime and Punishment" is a quintessential example of this genre, examining the psychological turmoil of its protagonist,

Raskolnikov, as he grapples with guilt and redemption. These stories provide a window into the complexities of human behavior, offering insights into the motivations and conflicts that drive individuals to act in seemingly irrational ways.

The exploration of psychological landscapes in literature is not limited to fiction; autobiographical works and memoirs also provide valuable insights into the human mind. Authors like Sylvia Plath and Maya Angelou have used their personal experiences to shed light on mental health issues, identity struggles, and the process of self-discovery. By sharing their journeys, these writers create a sense of connection and empathy, allowing readers to explore their own psychological landscapes in a meaningful way.

Ultimately, literature's ability to navigate the labyrinth of the mind underscores its power as a tool for psychological exploration and understanding. Through the diverse narratives and characters that populate the literary world, we gain valuable insights into the intricacies of the human psyche, enhancing our comprehension of ourselves and the cosmos.

5

Chapter 5: Cosmic Symbolism: The Universe in Metaphor

Symbolism has always been a powerful tool in literature, allowing writers to convey complex ideas and emotions through imagery and metaphor. When it comes to the cosmos, symbols and metaphors offer a way to make abstract concepts more accessible and relatable. From the ancient symbols of the zodiac to the modern representations of black holes and galaxies, cosmic symbolism provides a rich language for exploring the mysteries of the universe.

In classical literature, celestial bodies often symbolize divine or supernatural forces. The stars, for instance, have been used to represent fate and destiny, guiding characters on their journeys. Shakespeare's "Romeo and Juliet" famously opens with a reference to "star-crossed lovers," implying that their tragic fate is written in the stars. Similarly, the sun and the moon have been used to symbolize opposites—day and night, life and death, masculine and feminine energies. These symbols help to create a sense of cosmic order and meaning, connecting human experiences to the larger forces at play in the universe.

Modern literature continues to use cosmic symbolism to explore themes of existentialism and the nature of reality. In Jorge Luis Borges' short story "The Library of Babel," the universe is imagined as an infinite library containing all possible books. This metaphor serves as an exploration of the infinite possibilities and uncertainties of existence. The concept of parallel universes, popular in science fiction, also relies on cosmic symbolism to delve into questions of identity and choice. By using symbols to represent the cosmos, writers can create rich, multidimensional narratives that resonate on both a literal and metaphorical level.

Cosmic symbolism is not limited to literature; it also plays a significant role in psychology. Carl Jung's concept of the "cosmic unconscious" suggests that the symbols we use to describe the universe are deeply rooted in the collective unconscious. These symbols can serve as powerful tools for self-exploration and personal growth. By engaging with cosmic symbolism, individuals can gain insights into their own inner worlds and develop a deeper understanding of their place in the cosmos.

6

Chapter 6: The Interstellar Imagination: Science Fiction and the Human Condition

Science fiction has long been a genre that pushes the boundaries of imagination, exploring the farthest reaches of space and time. Through futuristic settings and speculative technologies, science fiction offers a unique lens through which to examine the human condition. By projecting our hopes, fears, and aspirations onto distant planets and advanced civilizations, science fiction provides a mirror that reflects the complexities of contemporary life.

One of the central themes in science fiction is the exploration of identity and what it means to be human. In Philip K. Dick's "Do Androids Dream of Electric Sheep?" (the basis for the film "Blade Runner"), the distinction between humans and artificial beings becomes increasingly blurred, raising questions about consciousness, empathy, and the essence of humanity. Similarly, Arthur C. Clarke's "2001: A Space Odyssey" explores the evolution of human intelligence and our relationship with technology, prompting readers to ponder the future trajectory of our species.

Science fiction also serves as a platform for social commentary, addressing issues such as inequality, oppression, and environmental degradation. In Octavia Butler's "Parable of the Sower," a dystopian future America serves as a backdrop for a story about resilience, community, and the search for a better world. Through these speculative narratives, science fiction offers a powerful critique of contemporary society and a vision of alternative futures.

The genre's capacity to envision the unknown allows for a deep exploration of existential questions. The vastness of space and the possibility of extraterrestrial life challenge our understanding of existence and our place in the universe. Works like Stanislaw Lem's "Solaris" and Ursula K. Le Guin's "The Left Hand of Darkness" delve into the nature of consciousness, communication, and the limits of human understanding. By imagining what lies beyond the familiar, science fiction encourages us to expand our horizons and embrace the unknown.

7

Chapter 7: The Cosmic Dance: Literature and Quantum Mechanics

The advent of quantum mechanics revolutionized our understanding of the universe, revealing a reality that is far stranger and more complex than previously imagined. Literature has responded to these scientific developments by incorporating themes of uncertainty, interconnectedness, and the nature of reality. Through the lens of quantum mechanics, writers have explored the fluid boundaries between fiction and reality, and the role of the observer in shaping the cosmos.

One of the key principles of quantum mechanics is the idea of superposition—the notion that particles can exist in multiple states simultaneously until observed. This concept has inspired literary works that blur the line between different realities and challenge our perception of time and space. For example, David Mitchell's "Cloud Atlas" weaves together multiple narratives across different time periods, suggesting a interconnected web of existence. The novel's structure reflects the quantum idea that all moments are interconnected and influence one another.

Another central concept in quantum mechanics is entanglement, where particles become interconnected in such a way that the state of one particle instantaneously affects the state of another, regardless of distance. This idea resonates with themes of interconnectedness and unity found in literature.

In Tom Stoppard's play "Arcadia," the characters' lives in different time periods are intricately linked through mathematics, poetry, and the natural world. The play explores how seemingly disparate events and individuals are connected through the fabric of the universe.

Quantum mechanics also challenges our understanding of reality, suggesting that the act of observation plays a crucial role in determining the state of the universe. This idea has profound implications for literature, where the reader's interpretation and perception shape the meaning of a text. Postmodern literature, with its emphasis on ambiguity and multiple perspectives, reflects this quantum view of reality. Works like Jorge Luis Borges' "The Garden of Forking Paths" invite readers to explore different possible outcomes and interpretations, highlighting the role of the observer in constructing meaning.

8

Chapter 8: The Poetry of the Stars: Celestial Imagery in Literature

The stars have long been a source of inspiration for poets and writers, serving as symbols of beauty, mystery, and transcendence. Celestial imagery in literature evokes a sense of wonder and awe, connecting human experiences to the vastness of the cosmos. Through the language of the stars, writers explore themes of love, longing, and the search for meaning.

In the works of Romantic poets like William Wordsworth and John Keats, the night sky becomes a canvas for exploring the sublime and the ineffable. Wordsworth's "Lines Written in Early Spring" captures the sense of interconnectedness between nature and the cosmos, while Keats' "Bright Star" uses the image of a steadfast star to symbolize eternal love and constancy. These poems reflect a deep reverence for the natural world and its connection to the greater universe.

Modern poets also draw on celestial imagery to convey complex emotions and ideas. In "The Love Song of J. Alfred Prufrock," T.S. Eliot uses the image of the evening sky "spread out against the sky / Like a patient etherized upon a table" to evoke a sense of alienation and disconnection. The stars in Eliot's poem become symbols of the fragmented and disenchanted modern world, highlighting the contrast between the vastness of the universe and the isolation of the individual.

Celestial imagery is not limited to poetry; it also plays a significant role in prose literature. In F. Scott Fitzgerald's "The Great Gatsby," the green light at the end of Daisy's dock serves as a symbol of Gatsby's unattainable dreams and the broader theme of the American Dream. The light, which can be seen as a distant star, represents the longing for something beyond reach, a desire that is both deeply personal and universal.

Through the use of celestial imagery, literature creates a sense of connection between the individual and the cosmos, reminding us of our place within the larger universe. The stars become a metaphor for the human experience, reflecting our hopes, dreams, and the mysteries that lie beyond our understanding.

9

Chapter 9: Dreams and the Night Sky: Unveiling the Subconscious

Dreams have long been a source of fascination and wonder, offering glimpses into the hidden recesses of the subconscious mind. Literature has often turned to the night sky and the cosmos as metaphors for the dream world, exploring the parallels between the vastness of space and the depths of the human psyche. By examining the interplay between dreams and the cosmos, we can uncover new insights into the mysteries of the mind.

In the realm of literature, dreams often serve as a narrative device to reveal characters' inner thoughts and emotions. In Shakespeare's "A Midsummer Night's Dream," the enchanted forest and the night sky create a dreamlike atmosphere where the boundaries between reality and illusion blur. The play explores themes of love, desire, and transformation, using the dream world as a space for characters to confront their subconscious fears and desires. Through this exploration, Shakespeare invites readers to consider the ways in which dreams shape our understanding of reality.

The connection between dreams and the cosmos is also evident in the works of Romantic poets like Samuel Taylor Coleridge and William Blake. Coleridge's "Kubla Khan" famously depicts a vision of a fantastical palace inspired by an opium-induced dream. The poem's vivid imagery and surreal landscapes evoke a sense of cosmic wonder, blurring the line between the dream world and the natural world. Similarly, Blake's "The Marriage of Heaven and Hell" explores the relationship between opposites, using celestial imagery to convey the interplay between light and darkness, reason and imagination.

In psychology, dreams are seen as a window into the unconscious mind, revealing hidden desires, conflicts, and unresolved issues. Carl Jung's theory of dreams suggests that they serve as a means of communication between the conscious and unconscious mind, providing valuable insights into the individual's inner world. By interpreting the symbols and themes that appear in dreams, individuals can gain a deeper understanding of their own psyche and the forces that shape their behavior.

The night sky, with its vast expanse and countless stars, serves as a powerful metaphor for the subconscious mind. Just as the cosmos contains hidden galaxies and distant worlds, the mind holds untapped potential and unexplored territories. By delving into the dream world, literature and psychology offer a path to self-discovery, revealing the intricate connections between the inner and outer worlds.

10

Chapter 10: The Language of the Universe: Symbols and Archetypes

The universe speaks to us in a language of symbols and archetypes, offering clues to its mysteries and our place within it. Literature and psychology have long recognized the power of these universal symbols to convey complex ideas and emotions. By decoding the language of the universe, we can gain new insights into the nature of reality and our own inner worlds.

Carl Jung's theory of archetypes suggests that certain symbols and themes are deeply embedded in the collective unconscious, resonating across cultures and epochs. These archetypes, such as the hero, the mentor, and the shadow, appear in literature as recurring characters and motifs. By examining these archetypal patterns, we can uncover the universal themes that shape human experience. For example, the hero's journey, as described by Joseph Campbell, mirrors the psychological process of personal growth and transformation. This narrative structure, found in myths and stories around the world, reflects the individual's quest for meaning and self-realization.

Literature is rich with symbols that convey the mysteries of the cosmos. In Herman Melville's "Moby-Dick," the white whale represents the unknown and the unattainable, a symbol of the vast and incomprehensible forces that govern the universe. Similarly, in Gabriel Garcia Marquez's "One Hundred

Years of Solitude," the recurring motif of the butterfly serves as a symbol of transformation and the passage of time. These symbols invite readers to explore the deeper layers of meaning within the text, offering a window into the complexities of the human experience.

The language of symbols is not limited to literature; it also plays a significant role in psychology. In dream analysis, symbols are seen as representations of unconscious thoughts and emotions. By interpreting the symbols that appear in dreams, individuals can gain insights into their own psychological processes and address unresolved issues. The symbols of the cosmos, such as stars, planets, and constellations, often appear in dreams as metaphors for the individual's journey through life.

Ultimately, the language of the universe offers a bridge between the inner and outer worlds, connecting the human experience to the larger forces at play in the cosmos. By engaging with symbols and archetypes, we can unlock new perspectives and deepen our understanding of ourselves and the universe.

11

Chapter 11: The Infinite Possibilities: Literature, Psychology, and Quantum Physics

Quantum physics has revolutionized our understanding of the universe, revealing a reality that is far more complex and interconnected than previously imagined. Literature and psychology have responded to these scientific advancements by incorporating themes of uncertainty, multiplicity, and the interconnectedness of all things. Through the lens of quantum physics, we can explore the infinite possibilities that shape our understanding of reality.

One of the key principles of quantum physics is the idea of superposition, which suggests that particles can exist in multiple states simultaneously until observed. This concept has inspired literary works that challenge traditional notions of time and space, creating narratives that explore parallel realities and alternative outcomes. For example, in Italo Calvino's "Invisible Cities," the narrator describes a series of fantastical cities that exist in different dimensions, each representing a different aspect of human experience. This structure reflects the quantum idea that all possibilities are interconnected and influence one another.

Another central concept in quantum physics is entanglement, where particles become interconnected in such a way that the state of one particle instantaneously affects the state of another, regardless of distance. This idea resonates with themes of interconnectedness and unity found in literature and psychology. In Alice Walker's "The Color Purple," the characters' lives are intricately linked through their shared experiences and struggles, highlighting the interconnectedness of human relationships. The novel's exploration of empathy and connection reflects the quantum view of reality as a web of interconnected possibilities.

Quantum physics also challenges our understanding of reality, suggesting that the act of observation plays a crucial role in determining the state of the universe. This idea has profound implications for literature, where the reader's interpretation and perception shape the meaning of a text. Postmodern literature, with its emphasis on ambiguity and multiple perspectives, reflects this quantum view of reality. Works like David Foster Wallace's "Infinite Jest" invite readers to explore different possible outcomes and interpretations, highlighting the role of the observer in constructing meaning.

By integrating the principles of quantum physics with literature and psychology, we can unlock new perspectives on the nature of reality and the infinite possibilities that shape our understanding of the cosmos. This interdisciplinary approach offers a rich tapestry of insights, revealing the interconnectedness of all things and the endless potential for discovery and growth.

12

Chapter 12: The Final Chapter: Reflecting on the Infinite Library

As we reach the final chapter of our exploration, we reflect on the journey we have undertaken through the infinite library of literature, psychology, and the cosmos. This journey has revealed the profound connections between these fields, highlighting the ways in which they decode the mysteries of the universe and the human experience.

Literature has served as a bridge between the known and the unknown, offering a space for imagination, reflection, and self-discovery. Through stories, symbols, and metaphors, literature has provided a rich language for exploring the complexities of the cosmos and our place within it. From ancient myths to modern science fiction, literary works have captured the wonder and awe of the universe, inviting readers to embark on their own journeys of exploration and understanding.

Psychology has deepened our understanding of the human mind, revealing the intricate landscapes of thought, emotion, and consciousness. By examining the psychological processes that underlie storytelling, we have gained insights into the ways in which literature shapes our perception of reality and our sense of self. The interplay between literature and psychology has illuminated the connections between the individual and the collective, the conscious and the unconscious, the inner and outer worlds.

The principles of quantum physics have further expanded our horizons, challenging traditional notions of reality and revealing the interconnectedness of all things. By integrating the concepts of superposition, entanglement, and the observer effect, we have explored the infinite possibilities that shape our understanding of the universe. This interdisciplinary approach has enriched our exploration, offering new perspectives on the nature of existence and the endless potential for discovery and growth.

As we close the final pages of "The Infinite Library: How Literature and Psychology Decode the Mysteries of the Cosmos," we are reminded that the journey of exploration and understanding is never truly complete. The universe, like the infinite library, holds endless possibilities and mysteries waiting to be discovered. Through literature, psychology, and the principles of quantum physics, we continue to unlock new insights and deepen our connection to the cosmos and ourselves.

13

Chapter 13: The Harmony of the Spheres: Music, Literature, and the Cosmos

Music, with its universal appeal and emotional resonance, has long been intertwined with literature and the cosmos. The concept of the "music of the spheres," dating back to Pythagoras, suggests that the movements of celestial bodies create a harmonious symphony that reflects the order of the universe. Literature has often drawn on musical themes and imagery to explore the relationship between sound, emotion, and the cosmos.

In classical literature, musical references abound, serving as metaphors for the harmony and disharmony of human experiences. In Shakespeare's "The Tempest," the ethereal music of Ariel creates an otherworldly atmosphere, symbolizing the magic and mystery of the island. Similarly, in Goethe's "Faust," the character of Mephistopheles uses music to seduce and manipulate, highlighting the power of sound to influence emotions and actions.

Modern literature continues to explore the connections between music and the cosmos. In Haruki Murakami's "Kafka on the Shore," music serves as a bridge between different realities, guiding characters through their journeys of self-discovery. The novel's blending of the surreal and the mundane reflects the idea that music, like the cosmos, transcends boundaries and unites disparate elements.

The psychological impact of music is well-documented, with studies showing its ability to evoke emotions, enhance memory, and foster social connection. By incorporating musical themes into literature, writers tap into these psychological effects, creating a richer and more immersive reading experience. The interplay between music, literature, and the cosmos invites readers to explore the harmonious connections that shape our understanding of the universe and ourselves.

14

Chapter 14: The Alchemy of Words: Literature and the Transformative Power of Language

Language is the alchemical force that transforms thoughts into words, emotions into poetry, and dreams into stories. Literature harnesses the power of language to create new worlds, evoke emotions, and explore the mysteries of the cosmos. By examining the transformative power of language, we can uncover the ways in which literature shapes our perception of reality and our understanding of the universe.

In literature, language serves as a vessel for conveying the ineffable, capturing the beauty and complexity of human experience. In James Joyce's "Finnegans Wake," the playful and experimental use of language reflects the fluid and multifaceted nature of consciousness. The novel's intricate wordplay and dense allusions create a tapestry of meaning that invites readers to explore the depths of the human mind.

The transformative power of language is also evident in the works of poets like Pablo Neruda and Rainer Maria Rilke. Neruda's odes and Rilke's elegies use language to capture the essence of existence, transforming ordinary experiences into moments of transcendence. Through their evocative imagery and lyrical expression, these poets reveal the profound connections between language, emotion, and the cosmos.

Psychology recognizes the impact of language on thought and behavior, with theories like the Sapir-Whorf hypothesis suggesting that language shapes our perception of reality. By engaging with diverse literary works, readers can expand their linguistic and cognitive horizons, gaining new perspectives on the world and their place within it. The alchemy of words allows literature to transcend boundaries and transform our understanding of the universe.

15

Chapter 15: The Cosmos Within: Inner Space and the Exploration of the Self

The exploration of the cosmos is not limited to the outer reaches of space; it also extends to the inner landscapes of the self. Literature and psychology have long been fascinated with the idea of "inner space," the vast and uncharted territory of the human mind. By delving into the depths of consciousness, literature offers a mirror that reflects the complexities of the self and the mysteries of existence.

In literature, the exploration of inner space often takes the form of introspective narratives and psychological explorations. Marcel Proust's "In Search of Lost Time" is a quintessential example of this genre, capturing the intricacies of memory, identity, and self-awareness. Through the narrator's reflections on his past, Proust creates a rich tapestry of inner experiences that mirror the complexity of the cosmos.

The concept of inner space is also central to the works of existentialist writers like Jean-Paul Sartre and Albert Camus. In Sartre's "Nausea," the protagonist's existential crisis and search for meaning reflect the vast and often disorienting nature of inner space. Camus' "The Stranger" explores themes of alienation and the absurd, highlighting the tension between the individual's inner world and the external universe.

Psychologically, the exploration of inner space is a journey of self-discovery and personal growth. Carl Jung's process of individuation, for instance, involves integrating the conscious and unconscious aspects of the self to achieve wholeness. Literature provides a valuable tool for this journey, offering insights into the complexities of the mind and the interconnectedness of all things.

As we navigate the cosmos within, we uncover the infinite possibilities that shape our understanding of the self and the universe. The exploration of inner space reveals the profound connections between literature, psychology, and the mysteries of existence, inviting readers to embark on their own journeys of discovery and transformation.

The Infinite Library, How Literature and Psychology Decode the Mysteries of the Cosmos

In "The Infinite Library: How Literature and Psychology Decode the Mysteries of the Cosmos," we embark on a fascinating journey through the realms of the imagination and reality. This book delves into the profound connections between literature, psychology, and the cosmos, revealing how these fields interweave to unlock the universe's most enigmatic secrets.

From ancient myths to modern science fiction, each chapter explores the rich tapestry of human experience, shedding light on the intricate dance between the mind and the cosmos. We discover how stories, symbols, and psychological insights offer a deeper understanding of the universe and our place within it.

Literature serves as a bridge between the known and the unknown, providing a space for imagination, reflection, and self-discovery. Psychology deepens our understanding of the human mind, revealing the intricate landscapes of thought, emotion, and consciousness. Together, they offer a rich language for exploring the complexities of the cosmos and our place within it.

"The Infinite Library" invites readers to explore the boundless possibilities of the cosmos and the limitless potential of the human imagination. Whether you are a lover of literature, a student of psychology, or a seeker of cosmic wisdom, this book provides a captivating and insightful journey through the infinite library of human knowledge and experience.

www.ingramcontent.com/pod-product-compliance
Lightning Source LLC
LaVergne TN
LVHW010443070526
838199LV00066B/6173